PANAMÁ
CROSSROADS OF THE WORLD
Reflections of Childhood

CARMEN BUELVAS CRITCHLOW

Carmen Critchlow

PANAMÁ
CROSSROADS OF THE WORLD
Reflections of Childhood

CARMEN BUELVAS CRITCHLOW

Acorn Publishing
A Division of Development Initiatives

PANAMÁ : CROSSROADS OF THE WORLD
Reflections of Childhood

© 2006 CARMEN BUELVAS CRITCHLOW

Published by Acorn Publishing
A Division of Development Initiatives
P.O. Box 84, Battle Creek, Michigan 49016-0084

Printed in the United States of America
First Edition, 2006

Cover graphics © Carmen Buelvas Critchlow & Jesse Baker

Library of Congress Cataloging-in-Publication Data

Critchlow, Carmen Buelvas, 1957-
  Panama, crossroads of the world : reflections of childhood / Carmen
Buelvas Critchlow.-- 1st ed.
     p. cm.
  ISBN 0-9774449-0-2 (soft cover)
  1. Critchlow, Carmen Buelvas, 1957---Childhood and youth. 2.
Panamanian Americans--Biography. 3. Panamanian Americans--Social
life and customs--20th century. 4. Panama--Social conditions--20th
century. 5. Immigrants--United States--Biography. I. Title.

  E184.P35C75 2006
  973'.046872870092--dc22

                              2005031983

ISBN 0-9774449-0-2

For current information about all releases by Acorn Publishing, visit our
web site: http://www.acornpublishing.com

I dedicate this book to all Buelvitas
and to my village and the people of Achiote, Panamá,
for all of the wonderful memories of childhood,
which have sustained me during my darkest moments.

Acknowledgements

Crisostomo Buelvas (my father)
Judith Urriola de Buelvas (my mother)

Buelvitas in order of birth:

Francisco Buelvas (Father's side)
Jose Rafael Casis (Mother's side)
Nickname Pibe
Judith Aurora Echanique (Mother's side)
Nickname Misia
Zarida Del Carmen Buelvas de Smith
Nickname Yayin
Roberto Antonio Buelvas
Nickname Don
Aminta Eneida Buelvas Hamm
Nickname Tita
Crisostomo Arnaldo Buelvas
Nickname Criso
Carmen Minerva Buelvas Critchlow
Ramon Omar Buelvas
Cecilia Isabel Buelvas Moyers
Zaira Maria Buelvas Ortega
Nickname Maity
Gloriela Imara Buelvas

CONTENTS

Early Memories of Youth

I was named Minerva Del Carmen Buelvas at birth. I was born deep in the jungles of Panamá at a place called Cañoquebrado belonging to the province of Colón. I was brought into the world by a 'partero' or midwife. It is not unusual for women to give birth at home with the aid of a midwife—either a man or a woman—and this practice continues even today.

When I was a few days old the thread from my umbilical cord came undone and I was bleeding. I was asleep by my mother's side when she woke up and noticed the blood. She checked herself and finding it was not from her she started to look me over and found that it was me. She related this story to me years later. She said that in that moment she prayed to Carmen, the patron saint of our nearest town, Achiote, offering that if she saved my life, then my name would be changed in her honor. My father, who was working in the field nearby, heard her screams and came in the house to find his wife and baby saturated in blood. When he saw where the blood was coming from he put a knife in the fire, and when it was red hot, he burned the belly button closed. At my baptism my name was changed to Carmen Minerva Buelvas, just as my mother had promised.

People say that children can't remember childhood memories before the age of five, but I have vivid memories of when I was very young. I cannot say how old, but much younger than five. I remember that we lived in a small wooden house, which I will call the house in the mountains. It was raised off the ground and there were five steps to the main living area for sleeping space. Our family cooked outside on an open fire. Because we did not have running water or electricity, we carried water from a nearby stream into the kitchen to wash the dishes. We used kerosene lamps for light. In the stream we also bathed and washed our clothes.

On each side of the house we grew lemon grass, which we used to make tea for breakfast. Breakfast consisted of boiled bananas or yucca (a root, similar to a potato), and fried plantains or an elephant ear, which was made with flour, salt, egg and water, resembling a tortilla. Breakfast often included an egg patty, because we raised chickens, or fried fish. With this meal we also drank either coffee or lemon grass tea with milk and sugar.

We lived on a farm abundant with animals. We had a pig tied to an enormous guava tree right in front of the house. In addition to the pigs and chickens we also had ducks, horses and cows, as well as a big yellow dog that helped us to herd the cows. We drank the milk from the cows and our father made cheese. He would let the milk set until it curdled and would then place it on a wooden mold press and leave it over night. This process squeezed the extra fluid from the substance. When it was finished we had a wonderful white, salty-tasting cheese, which we ate at breakfast. Sometimes Father would place a tablet in the milk and make yellow cheese.

Our father and my older siblings, Yayin, Roberto and Criso, picked coffee all day long. I would sit on the last step of the house waiting for their return. I watched the pig tied to the guava tree go around and around, getting all tangled until he had no more room to go anywhere and needed help getting untangled. I suppose that my job was to untangle him so he would not choke to death on the rope. I remember that all the other animals ran loose around the farm, but this particular pig was very malicious to everyone. He attacked and bit anyone who came near him, although for some reason he liked me.

Since we lived in the jungle, we did not have any close neighbors. We could walk for miles before seeing any other living soul. Our family owned sixty acres of land. Coffee was the primary crop, but we also grew plantains, bananas, coconut, oranges, grape-fruit, breadfruit, lemons, limes, cocoa, sugar cane and other crops that I can't even name. We carried this produce by canoe, horses or by foot to the main roads, so that we could take it to the city of Colón to sell. With the money we got for the produce we bought staple foods like sugar, rice, flour, cooking oil, kerosene for lamps and other things we could not grow in our lush corner of the jungle.

When we traveled with our produce to market it took many days, so the journey had to be accomplished in stages. The first step was to load the horses and canoe. Father made packing saddles for the horses out of wood, resembling a miniature teepee. To protect the horses' flesh, my father lined the saddles with padding on the inside, which he made of dry reeds. We packed the burlap coffee sacks on either side of the saddle. When space allowed, a small child rode on top. Our mother usually led the first horses and the others just followed. As children we walked with our mother with whatever we could carry in a basket made of reeds. These hand-made baskets were placed on our backs and attached to our foreheads with a strap.

Father and Roberto were in charge of the canoe, which was full of fruit and vegetables. They were responsible for getting their load to the next stage. Although this journey took many hours, Father usually completed this stage first and then sometimes walked back to meet us. He was always concerned for the children and also for the horses, not wanting to tire any of us out. Even though Father was hard-working and expected the same from his family, he also knew not to push the horses, himself or us to exhaustion. When we reached the second stage we stayed overnight at a ranch-style house we had halfway between the nearest town and the coffee farm. This, which I will call the house by the llanos (marsh), was also made of wood with a tin roof. It had one large room with a kitchen on one end, living quarters in the center and sleeping quarters on the opposite end.

The trail between the first and second stages was always wet and muddy and so narrow that we had to walk one behind the other. Usually the dog led the way, then Mother, horses, and children followed. Very rarely did we see anyone on this trail. Behind this house was the river that carried my father's canoe full of produce. He would tie it up on the bank below the house and wait until morning to continue to the third stage.

It was in this river that my mother taught us girls the proper way to wash clothes. She made this work a game. We went to the edge of the river near a large flat rock, which we used, along with a tin wash tub, wash board, bar of soap and a brush, to rub and scrub the clothes. We always washed the white clothes first because they were to be soaked in soapy water. Without being wrung out they were placed on a zinc sheet in a sunny spot to be bleached by the sun. By the time we finished washing the rest of the clothes the whites were done. While we washed the clothes we also played and swam. When we finished we hung them on a cloth line tied to the grapefruit tree on one end and a house post on the other.

The river was a source of life, but also could be a source of death. As a small child my brother Criso almost drowned there. He was in the canoe with my mother, and as she was rowing she did not see him fall out. It was fortunate that she looked back when she heard a muffled noise. She was able to grab him before he was submerged. The same river was our friend in calm times, when we spent countless hours playing within its banks, yet was transformed into our dark enemy during torrential tropical rains.

When it overflowed the river's current towed everything from its path and carried it downstream. After the rains stopped my father took the boys in the canoe and looked for the narrowings, which were made by the tree trunks and mud. They cleaned them, as it was an unspoken rule that anyone who lived along the banks should act as caretakers, so that the river would remain free-flowing for everyone to travel on as safely as possible.

The next stage of the journey took us to the village of Achiote. This trail was very different from the first. Part of the way was "llanos" (marshy), but most of the way it was a grassy open field, which was dry. Here the smaller children who didn't have anything to carry could run and play. Along the way we could see my father on the river; we waved and tried to race him to the landings close to the river, where we could just talk to him as he rowed. Then he moved further down the river where he was hidden by the jungle. We were not able to see him again until we arrived at our destination, where we all unloaded the canoes and the horses. After being unburdened at the front door, the horses were allowed to roam free.

Two-Story House

In the village of Achiote, the last stage before reaching the city of Colón, yet another house offered us shelter. This was our permanent residence. It was different from the other two houses, for this was our home.

It was a two-story structure, made of wood with a roof of zinc sheets. The downstairs was open with a spacious kitchen and a round table where we all sat and shared our meals. Our food was prepared over a large raised fire pit at one end of the kitchen.

A family room and an extra room on the side was a place for hanging the laundry on rainy days and where there was a small bed in case we had visitors. Not everyone had more than two houses. Sometimes, a friend would come from the mountains to bring his crop to trade or sell, or just to visit. If visitors needed a place to stay, we always let them use this extra room. It was a rule in our house that we set a plate of food from dinner aside in case someone hungry showed up unexpectedly.

The floor in the kitchen and the living room was

made of cement. The extra room was packed, hard dirt, which my father taught me how to sweep. I remember once my mother told me to sweep the house. When my father saw me sweeping with the random motions of a child, he took the broom from me and showed me to sweep a space and then step in the clean space and sweep away from me. When cleaning the dirt floor, which had its own challenges, my father instructed me to sweep very lightly in order to take away the "dirty" dirt and leave the "clean" dirt.

The second story of our home was raised off the ground quite high with about twenty steps leading upstairs. The upstairs was enclosed and included a large porch, a spacious family room, and a smaller kitchen in the back of the family room with a second set of stairs. To the right of the family room we had three bedrooms. The reason the house was so high with a kitchen upstairs is that during the rainy season it would flood. The first floor of the house would sometimes be under water and we would have to do the living upstairs.

Right outside of the house we had a wide yard where my father built an impressive teeter-totter that also went round and round. The boys climbed on one side and the girls balanced on the other. My father pushed us in the warm afternoon sun. When he was not available to perform his pushing duty, we just teeter-tottered on our own. Or, Roberto pushed us until we were dizzy and became sick to our stomachs.

Ours was the only house on this lot. Although the lot next to us was not ours, it was empty and we also played there. Coconut palms divided the lots. We liked to cook rice with the coconut milk, so we often let the coconuts on several palms get dry. When the meat of the coconut hardened, we used a grater that my father made out of tin to shave the coconut into fine pieces. After the coconut was grated we soaked it in water and used the same grater as a colander to drain the water, which we then used to cook the rice. The fruit from the other palms we ate while they were green. When the coconut is green, the meat is very soft and the water inside is incredibly sweet.

Across the road from the front of the house stood a steep hill. This hill was layered with boulders that came loose during the rainy season. When the rains fell, the boulders would shift and just roll down the hill, sometimes coming very close to our house. Although we never had one hit our house, one massive rock once landed right next to us.

Behind the house by the upstairs kitchen stairs my father built a seven-barrel "water tower" to bring water into the house. This water collector filled when it rained, and its supply would last a long time. Ours was the only house in town with "indoor water" for cooking and doing dishes. From that same water tower we drew water to bathe in the morning and evening. A short distance from this tower we had two outhouses.

From the porch of our home I could watch a living

fence come to life. My mother planted roses, along with red and white hibiscus, between the house and the road. From these plants she took clippings and put them in the ground, where they almost magically sprouted to life. Along our property from the hibiscus to the river we planted a silk worm tree fence. This tree has spikes from its base to its branches. My father cut the limbs of the tree and planted them closely together, forming a very tight, living fence. The spikes created a natural barrier that prevented the animals from getting out. It seemed that the fence multiplied and flourished overnight.

Panamá's weather is very humid. With temperatures between 60 and 90 degrees F. all year long, growing plants is easy. From the porch I also watched the many species of birds that came to rest in the hibiscus. Images still linger in my mind of a slough moving slowly across the road and sometimes people walking by.

All of us children had a hand in building our two-story house. I used to climb the ladder and cross the rafters to bring nails and water to the workers. I remember falling off the rafters. I hit the ground so hard that I lost my breath. But that did not stop me from climbing right back up again. In our family we were not allowed to show weakness; we picked ourselves up, dusted off, put it behind us and continued our work.

In the evenings by the light of the lamp our father

read to us. When I was old enough I sat in the middle of the stairs and read aloud to the others, whoever was in the house. People told my mother how much they enjoyed it. Upstairs my mother had a pedal sewing machine where she sat for hours making dresses for us girls. Or she ironed our school clothes with a heavy iron she put on the burning wood in the fireplace to absorb heat.

At Christmas time our family displayed a large Nativity scene with all sorts of miniature animals on a broad table on the porch. People often came to admire it. My mother was a great singer, so each year we gathered around her as she initiated the Christmas songs. As the guests left they dropped a coin in a dish that was placed next to the baby Jesus. These coins were then used to buy a new piece to expand the Nativity scene each succeeding year.

One rainy season when I couldn't sleep, I listened to the rain falling on the roof of the house. If everything was quiet it sounded like eggs or meat frying on a pan. I could also hear the frogs or insects singing and the monkeys howling far away. I loved this house where Ramón, Cecilia, Maity and Gloriela were born. And in this very same house my baby sister Gloriela died.

My earliest memories of both deep joy and deep sorrow are bound to that house and those people I love.

Going Hunting

When we returned home from the long journey we chose our part of the fruits and vegetables. The rest was traded to the people in town who had fruits or vegetables that we did not have. This was common practice because sometimes neither family had, but everyone always had something to offer. If they did not have food or goods to trade, they performed some kind of labor in exchange.

Before taking the coffee to the city to sell we had to dry it. When we were in town, our mother's job, along with the younger children, was to take great care in the important task of drying the coffee beans. Drying coffee is a long and laborious process. The coffee is picked by hand when the berries are red and ripe. It wasn't too bad when the weather was dry, but when it rained the ants and spiders seemed to hear their own invitation to join in the activity. We had to put our hands along each branch to pick every red bean, no matter how many multi-legged creatures were ready to compete. Just let me say that it wasn't fun when it was wet. The drying process took weeks. We would spread the coffee out on a cement slab or tarpaulin in the hot sun. The coffee had to be turned every hour. When night came we packed it up and in the morning continued the process. We could not let the coffee get wet, because it would mold, and the crop would be lost for the season. We repeated this procedure for weeks until the coffee was finally dried.

All of the town's people helped each other with this task. When the drying process was finally completed, all of the families with coffee to sell gathered together and took it into the city of Colón to the coffee house. Usually, it was the "Casa Duran" that bought the coffee. After we sold our coffee and the crop was all finished for the season, our father took us hunting—another adventure.

Father had a rifle, which we were not allowed to touch. The only exception was my sister, Yayin, because she was older. To include us in the hunting tasks, he showed us children how to make slingshots. We used a length of wood that resembled a Y, a piece of inner tube from an old tire or rubber bands—or sometimes elastic. We then tied it to each side of the top of the Y, making the sides and a holding pocket formed of rubber.

This was a weapon; as such, we were never permitted to just play with the tool. You were only to use it to kill what you were going to eat. During the day we hunted birds, rabbits, ñeque (an animal similar to a rabbit but much bigger), squirrels, iguanas, or iguana eggs. Sometimes, we came across caiman eggs. Caimans are in the family of crocodile. We cooked the eggs like regular chicken eggs. We carried stones to put in the slingshots. We all had excellent aims and shot right to the temple. We usually had a kill of small animals on our very first shots.

My father taught us how to track prey by its scent. He had us bite down on a leaf from a special plant. It made our tongues numb and it heightened our sense of smell, so that tracking the animal was much easier. Iguanas were more difficult to track because sometimes they hid in the water. We had to go into the water in order to find them, or wait them out. When we did go in the water, we had to be careful how we handled them. If you held the tail wrong, the tail could break off, allowing the iguana to get away. Still, most of the time we made a catch.

If we became thirsty while hunting and there was not a stream or clean water nearby, our father cut a hole in one of a special palm tree. The inside of this tree was full of a sweet tasting fluid our father called wine. The hole in the palm tree seemed to seal very quickly, because when we returned a week later it was closed. Again we were able to drain the fluid from it and quench our thirst.

Our father taught us to kill, clean and cook our catch. At night we went hunting for mud turtles. He also taught us how to catch, clean and cook fish. We used bread crumbs to lure the fish to the surface. Among the crumbs we had a hook hidden and tied to a string on a short stick. Night was the time to hunt for eggs, laid by turtles, which were about six to ten inches in length. The children were not allowed to do this, because it was dangerous. Usually my father and other men in the village did the turtle hunting, but we were permitted to come along. The men poked the mud with sticks. If it sounded hard, they reached their hands into the mud and caught the turtle. Enough were always caught to host a big town-wide cookout. If we were tired from the hunt, our mother cleaned and cooked whatever we brought home. We had to cook everything we caught right away, because we did not have refrigeration to preserve it. We tried to never catch more than we could eat; if we did, we shared with other families.

Our mother would eat almost everything we caught, except iguana. She said, "I won't eat lizard," but she did enjoy iguana eggs. Iguana eggs are very small, about the size of a robin's egg. We would boil them and string them out on the clothes line to dry until they were very hard. We then put them in soup or ate them dry.

Our everyday meals were the same. For lunch it was soup to which we added left-over rice from the day before. Rice was one of the few foods we could leave outside of the refrigerator without it spoiling. Our father always said that without soup he could not survive. For dinner we ate rice with some kind of bean and whatever meat we had caught for the day, sometimes fish or chicken. We always had enough food and never worried about going hungry.

In our village none of the other girls ever went hunting, because that was not considered "lady-like." Our father said that he taught us girls all the same things the boys learned because he wanted his daughters to be self-sufficient, and not to depend on anyone if we didn't want to. My father's main trade was architecture. He was a mason, so he also taught us how to mix sand, gravel and cement and make a mold to form bricks. Today, I would be lost without my cement, plaster and paint.

My father taught all of his children to be survivors. I am very grateful to him for that life learning.

Achiote

Other than the river as a means of transportation, only one road brought people in and out of my village of Achiote. For days, no one came or went. Occasionally two or three cars drove by in one day. Although we were relatively isolated from outside civilization, all the families knew one another and helped each other out.

Our village had two wooden bridges with surfaces covered in tar. We had to cross one of these on our way to school. In the afternoon when we returned for the afternoon shift, my older brother Roberto carried us, one by one, across since we didn't wear shoes to school. In this village we didn't have to wear uniforms, because most of the families in the village couldn't afford to buy them, especially with so many kids. My brothers, sisters and I had three sets of clothing. On Sundays or special days we wore our good clothes. For ordinary days we had school clothes and play clothes. When we went out to play, we'd better remember which clothes to wear. Shoes were optional. Since each of us had only one pair, when we stopped and played under the bridge we didn't want to ruin them in the mud and water. Walking across the bridge in the hot sun was impossible, because the tar was so hot it burned our feet. Roberto was tough and ran very fast across with one of us on his back. He made the trip time after time until all of us were on the other side.

Our village was home to about 50 families. All of them had about the same number of children. There was a main road and in the middle of town another road curved to the right from the school house, leading to the cemetery. It seemed like a very far away, dreadfully scary place. Most of the time it was overgrown by the jungle. It was often hard to find the family graves because they were marked with stick crosses, which sometimes fell down and rotted before we could come fix them. When we went to clean and maintain the graves, often we could not find the grave markers.

There were three small stores where families could go to the counter and ask for what was needed. The storekeepers had a notebook where they wrote your name down if you didn't have money to pay right away. Usually, it was the end of harvest season before they could be paid.

The bridge closer to our house is where we went to wash the laundry and swim. I remember that I learned to swim in this river. All of my older siblings knew how to swim but I didn't, so one day when my father went with us, I pleaded with him to teach me. Usually, he brought a rope so that he could tie it around our waist to pull us across the river while we tried to swim. This time he didn't have one and got tired of my asking him. He just threw me in. He said I could either "swim or drown." I didn't want to drown, so I swam. Deep down I knew my father would not let me drown, but being a young child I was scared. All my brothers were laughing at me and told me to keep my head above water. They yelled, "That's the way we learned to swim."

I also learned about marriage by watching life around me. I saw some of the older girls in our village marry older widowed men. These men had children with their first wives and then soon, together with the girls, they would have more children. I could see changes in the girls after they were married. Assuming so much responsibility taking care of all those children, they appeared to have grown into women over night. I also saw men beat their wives, and I knew I did not want to live that kind of life. I knew that if I married one of those men, it would be a matter of "kill or be killed," and I was not going to be the one to be killed. I was not going to let myself be abused.

My mother taught us that we were supposed to care for our husbands and they would take care of us. I knew that "taking care of" did not mean suffering abuse at their hands.

In our home village my father taught us how to ride a horse. Our horses were primarily used for cargo, carrying coffee or produce from the farm to the town. When we took the horses back to the farm, usually only one was fully loaded. Each of us would be on a horse, as we rode them along the riverbank, the plains or on the "llanos" (marshes). We sang as we traveled along and tried to make our horses dance as they did in the Mexican movies. Sometimes, we pretended that we were riding on our own "Ponderosa," like we saw on television. We were allowed to visit some close friends of my mother who lived on the other side of town. They had a generator for electricity and an operating television. Every Sunday night they let us come over to watch *Bonanza*.

Our horses were trained to come to the sound of a whistle, and to go home on their own. In Achiote, I learned about life and death. Our father took care of the medical needs of his animals, the same as ours. He was known as the "teacher" because, although he was not a medicine man, he knew how to mix all of his oils as a cure-all.

Our father had his own crude but efficient methods of curing our ills. He had oils of all kinds to aid him. I remember many jars of alligator oil, snake oil, turtle oil, castor oil, fish oil, whale fat oil, and I don't know what other oils. Though I don't remember what conditions they cured or were used for, he had one concoction call "Tiro Seguro." I didn't learn the ingredients, but I knew very well what it did. Our father gave each of his children a tablespoon of this foul-tasting oil once a month to de-worm us, just like he did to his animals.

I didn't want to drink that stuff until my friend, Helena, was taken ill. She had a twin brother and they were always with us playing together. One morning she did not feel well and her mother kept her indoors for days. When her father came over to get my father to see what he could do, it was too late. We all came running. My father told us children to go home, but before he could stop me I took a peek inside. There was my little friend shriveled in her bed. Her face was gray and worms were coming from her nose, mouth and ears. Never in my life had I seen such horror. Not even my father could save her. Those worms had choked the life out of her. I lost a friend forever. After that I always took the concoction my father gave us, because I knew it might save our lives.

I also remember the cures he had for cuts and wounds. I recall him using a sewing needle on our older brother's leg. My two older brothers, Roberto, Criso, and I were far from home cutting wood when Roberto hit his shin with the ax right below the knee, almost through to the bone. Criso and I had to carry him bleeding all the way home. When my father saw us carrying our brother he rushed to us, took him from our arms and carried him the rest of the way and into the house. He took coffee grounds and packed the wound to stop the bleeding. He then used a needle and sewed the wound closed.

Sometimes when a wound was not deep, our father burned it shut. He put the knife on the fire until it was red hot; then in a quick movement he placed it flat on the wound and took it fast away. He also sewed his own wounds when needed, or had someone else do it for him. I remember once when he cut his hand, he could not sew the wound on his own. No one else in the family had the nerve to do it so he said it was up to me to help him. He showed me how he wanted me to sew. After pouring some rum on the open wound and on the needle and thread he told me to do as he had shown me, so I sewed it shut. I was not afraid; I just wanted my dad to be ok. I suppose that by today's standards my father's "cures" for us might be considered abuse. However, I know that our father did everything possible to save our lives, because trying to get to the nearest hospital could take all day. By then, the life could be lost.

Discipline

I have to say that my mother was a perfectionist, and she expected no less than that of her children. As her children, we were admired for our behavior, respectful manners, and for the way we showed respect to others. Our mother and father had zero tolerance for disrespect and misbehavior. We were Buelvitas, children of Mr. Buelvas, and we were expected to conduct ourselves as such. You did not disrespect that name. Although sometimes we were physically punished, our parents had that "look," and many times all it took was that "look" for us to know that it was time to behave. In public you behaved as if your parents were with you. If anyone in the village told my parents of our bad behaviors, punishment was harsh.

I remember when my mother sent me to the store to buy a can of sardines for dinner. I stopped along the way to play with my brothers and some friends. I lost track of what I was supposed to do and lost the money. Going to the store our family used, I told the lady that my mother wanted a can of sardines and to put it on the list. My mother did not like to buy anything on credit. She did not like to owe anyone money. She always said that she would rather go without than to owe anyone. Anyway, the lady gave me a serious look and asked me if I was sure my mother had sent me. "Yes," I said, so she gave me the sardines. A period of time went by, and the lady asked my mother when she was going to pay her bill. I had never seen my mother so upset. She said she had never been so humiliated and embarrassed in her life. She didn't even know she owed the money. She told me I was to never again do a thing like that to her or anyone else. Needless to say, I received deserved punishment.

I also remember one day after our mother had gotten a new cistern. A cistern is a very heavy clay jar used as a container for holding water. It has a matching lid to keep the water fresh for drinking. Before leaving for work, our mother told us not to touch the cistern. Of course, my little brother Ramón had to touch it. The jar was placed on a high stool, but Ramón managed to reach up and pull it down. The cistern came crashing down to the ground in what seemed like a million pieces. Volumes of water flowed all over the place. Minutes before my mother walked in the door, my little brother stood guilty and soaked to the skin. She did not have to ask who did it. She could see that. We all knew what the punishment would be. Before my mother could react, that little boy ran past her and out the door. He was gone all day. Many hours later, there came Ramón along with Father. Ramón was wearing our father's underwear tied on the waist with a rope. We could not help but laugh at the sight. My mother came to see what was so funny, and she also broke out in laughter. Ramón's punishment was forgotten for that day.

When my mother went to the city she always brought us a large peppermint candy or sugar cookies to share. She first checked the house to make sure it was clean and everything was in its place and then checked to make sure all her children were accounted for before she gave us our reward. Her explanation was simple: "I know how much you fight when I am not here—and you could have killed each other." Although our mother was very harsh with us when we needed discipline, she was also generous and rewarded us when it was deserved. Although, it was also true that with her we got away with more than with our father. My father was different; he never physically punished us. He just gave us the "look," and we immediately knew that he meant business.

Folklore, Superstition or Religion

In the country of Panamá superstition and religion go hand in hand. Perhaps it is sometimes easier to be superstitious than to explain the unexplainable. In my Panamá and from my perspective as a child, superstition and religion were one and the same.

Once, while we were working in the house by the llanos, a poisonous viper bit my father. People said that it was placed on his path because someone was jealous of our family. People around town said that an "evil" woman knew magic spells to alter events in others' lives. They said she could make someone fall in love, hurt another at will, or even get rid of unwanted persons. It became common belief in our community that this woman had put a curse on our family and that from that day on a black karma would follow us and all our generations to come.

It was said that the viper that bit our father was native to Africa, one of the most venomous snakes of all. In order for that snake to be on our property, someone had to have placed it there. When bitten by this snake, if you didn't die instantly you could bleed to death from every orifice, open wound or pore in your body. Our father was bitten on one of his big toes. He immediately cut it open to bleed the poison out, but the poison was already in the bloodstream when my mother found him.

For days, while my mother fought her way through the jungle by canoe to civilization and the nearest hospital, my father continued to bleed. It was said that the person who planted the snake on our father's path must have thrown it in the cold river. Otherwise, our father would not have gotten the side effects he had after returning home from his long hospital stay. It was common knowledge in my village that if you were to bury the dead snake and had the good fortune to survive, there would be no side effects. Our father had side effects.

The lingering side effects he suffered were to his mind, but they had grave effects on his body and his life. He could no longer go to either the house on the mountain or the llanos. Now he could no longer work on the farm. Every time he set foot there, his body went into some kind of frenzy. His face became distorted and he just could not function. Our mother said he had become allergic to the jungle.

With our father disabled in this way, even though we were still children, we had to run the farm without him. As hard as we struggled through the long growing season, it became clear that this arrangement was not working out for our family. Even though he hired people to help, we just could not do the work our father did. Although he attempted time and again to go to the farm, he had severe reactions that endangered his health each time.

One day our father left the house without telling anyone. Hours later, his horse returned without him. We knew he had gone to the farm and that something bad had happened to him. After following the trail we found Father in the river with his machete lodged in his leg. He said he had had one of his "allergic reactions," fell off the horse, and could not gather the strength to remount. So, he sent the horse home to get help. We put him on his horse and took him home. Of course, after getting him home he just cleaned his cut, sewed it up and then went on as if nothing had happened. From then on he did not go to the farm, but stayed in the two-story house in Achiote.

In Panamá, when a baby is born, a red string is tied to the wrist or ankle of the infant. It's said that this was done to protect them from evil. When you are older there is a sea bean called a "Matc" that is made into a necklace for the same purpose. My mother believed in these superstitions. She tied the red string to my little sister Gloriela's wrist, but this did not help to chase away the "evil spirits."

One day our little sister was happily playing; the next day she was gone. Our mother said someone had been giving her the "evil eye." According to my mother, if a person with bad karma looked at another person wrong, especially infants, it could give them the "evil eye." And if you didn't call the "curandero" right away, the baby could die. A curandero in the Panamanian culture is a medicine man. So by the time she went to get him to dispel the "evil" from the baby and he arrived, our baby sister had died.

Our father built her coffin. In small towns like ours the men always built the coffins for their dead. A wake was observed. All the mirrors in the house were covered. This was to prevent the baby's soul fom getting trapped inside. A novena followed, with its nine-day prayer ritual to aid the soul to heaven. And then our lives were empty.

It seemed that from that day forward nothing was the same. We went about our daily chores. Life went on, but without much enthusiasm. It was as if torn shreds of heart flesh had been ripped out of us, leaving each of us numb. This was my mother's last baby. Because my mother believed in this curse, she was always worried that more of her children would be torn from her. She lived in fear that the "tulivieja" (Boogie-Woman) that hid in the woods would come out at night to steal her children. This Boogie-Woman would take the children and give them to the gnomes that lived far inside the jungle.

She also told us that if we went out by the river by ourselves, the "llorona" would steal us away. We have this legend about a woman called the "Crier" (la llorona) who took her baby to the river to bathe and for some reason it drowned. So this so-called "llorona" comes out and steals the babies from women who don't take good care of their children. Of course this is not true, but when you are a child, you believe what your parents tell you.

This is all superstition, just as when they warn you to turn your broom upside down by the entrance of the home, so the witches won't come in. Or, if you come in after midnight, you must walk though the front door backwards, so that the evil spirits don't follow you in. Or, if you sleep with your clothes inside out, the witches won't bother you in your sleep. Or, don't ever go swimming on Good Friday, because you will turn into a fish. We found out that this was not true, when on that very day my mother lay down and told us to play quietly. When she fell asleep, we snuck out to the river and went swimming. When we came home, she knew where we had been and each one of us got a spanking. Or, don't let the men go to the river right before dawn, because the siren will seduce them and they will never return. I also remember that when we lost a tooth, we were told to throw it on the roof so the mice would take it and bring a new one. These were some of the many superstitions that wove through my childhood like the warp in a wool blanket.

In South and Central American countries every town has a patron saint. We celebrate that day with a procession and a big party afterwards. The procession started in the church right after the Mass, and continued to a certain point in the village and then back to the church.

The singing and chanting took hours to complete, because the carriers of the Saint always took a few steps forward and a few steps back. Then they again took three steps forward and two back, and so on. This represented life, with its ebb and flow. Sometimes, life can be wonderful (the steps forward) and other times, tragedy happens and you have hardships (the steps back). With all of this the Saint was not returned to the church until well past midnight.

I don't remember the church ever being open to just come in and sit. We were told that if you left the doors of the church open, the lost souls would come into the church at night for refuge. Once, when a neighbor who owned one of the stores close to our house died, the family took him to the church. I guess he had gone hunting alone. The hour was getting really late and when he had still not returned, his wife came over to get my father to see if he would help her sons search for him. They found him under a massive fallen tree. They brought him home in the back of their truck, his body all bloody and torn up.

I was afraid to go in the church. My mother and other ladies said that I had to go in and touch the corpse, and then I would not be scared of the dead. And besides, they said he wouldn't come back and pull my foot at night. When I finally went inside, the body

36

was surrounded by candles. The church with all its strange scents and reminders of death was just not a pleasant place to be. To this day candles turn me off.

We also had a celebration every second day of November called the Day of the Dead. "Dia de los Muertos" or All Soul's Day. Everyone in town goes to the cemetery to clean, take flowers, and pay respect to the dead ancestors. Most members of the family take their machetes and spend much of the day there cleaning and grooming the tomb sites and reminiscing about when that family member was with us. Some of the men also bring their liquor and drink to their dead, but before they take a drink they pour some on the grave as remembrance and out of respect for that person.

I recall one lady who lived with her little boy near the school. She immersed her St Martin de Porres, a patriot saint, upside down in a glass of water whenever she lost the lottery. She said this was to punish him. When she won, she brought him out again and lit a candle to pay respect until the next time.

Although Panamanians are mostly Catholic, in my village we also had a Baptist church. It was a place of curiosity for some of us who didn't understand. From the road we could hear the people yelling and often wondered what in the world was going on inside. One day I was invited to go along, so my little sister Maity and I went. I was scared, because I was told that the Baptists didn't have saints or altars and that the devil hid behind the red curtain in the front. I wanted to know if this was true, so I kept my eyes fixed on the red curtain. When the service was over I sneaked a peek behind the curtain. I don't know if I was disappointed or relieved, but I saw no devil. All that my bulging eyes spotted was water for the baptism. I had to go home with a report to the rest of the family of what I witnessed. I began to understand how superstitions, half-truths, and ungrounded fears build invisible walls, which alienated people from one another.

I learned about God from the nuns who came every couple of years to teach us the Catechism. This is the rule book for youngsters between nine and eleven to memorize in order to prepare for First Communion. Before First Communion you are not allowed to partake of the sacraments. The nuns stayed as long as it took for all of us in that age group to learn our Catechism and partake of this important sacrament. Then they were gone for several years.

We did not have a priest that stayed in our village. A visiting priest came once a month for Mass or for funerals and special patron's day celebrations. Otherwise, the church was closed. On those special Sundays my mother sometimes went to church, but my father only participated in the processions and other religious celebrations. He did not attend church regularly. He said that most people who went to church were hypocrites, because on Sundays they were confessing and repenting their sins, but Monday through

Saturday they were taking the Lord's name in vain or didn't lend a helping hand to someone in need. He believed that a real Christian was someone who helped his neighbor every day. He chose to worship the Lord in his own way. I know he was not a Jehovah's Witness, but I remember him reading the Watchtower that someone brought him.

Jehovah's Witnesses seemed to materialize from nowhere. I thought they had spies all over because no matter where we lived or how remote our village was, they always found us. I laugh to myself every time I think of these things I was told as a child and believed. When I go home now from time to time I still hear these same stories.

So, don't sleep with your feet pointing towards the door, because you will be pulled out and your soul will be left behind. And definitely do not go to the church after dark, for you don't know what souls are lurking there.

Grandmother

W hen our mother was growing up she had to be perfect, because her mother required it of her. I did not like our Grandmother Zaira. Our grandmother was very cruel to our mother and to us children. She did not like us.

Our mother was the youngest of six children. Her older sister, Eneida, was a nurse. The following sister, Aminta, was married to a military man and lived overseas in Spain. The three brothers were dead. In the 1950s and '60s tuberculosis was rampant and it took many lives, including my youngest uncle.

Our mother's older brother, Roberto, was shot to death on the steps of the "Casa Blanca," the equivalent of the White House. He was a well-known reporter who had written articles against the government. As I was told, the President's brother assassinated my Uncle Roberto. This was a very difficult time for our grandmother, since this brother had been working to support her family. Even though the family knew who shot him, the assassin was never brought to trial. His punishment for murder was an Ambassadorship to

Spain. The third brother, who had married and lived outside the city, also died leaving a wife and children behind.

Now my mother was the youngest. Our grandmother never got over these tragic losses, since she had also lost her husband not long before her sons. Maybe these tragedies affected her disposition and attitude towards us, her grandchildren. None of us children were close to our grandmother, because of the way she treated us as we were growing up. She was a very domineering woman and always got her way, no matter what. My mother was the outlet for her disappointment and rage.

Usually, when my mother went to visit her, she took only one child at a time, because my grandmother did not like what she called "misbehaving kids" in her home. She sat us at the kitchen table, gave us a piece of bread and a cup of tea with milk, and told us not to leave crumbs on her table. We were not to move and definitely not to touch anything, while in the meantime she and my mother went in the bedroom to "talk." After they finished their "talk," my mother would be crying. Then she was depressed for days.

Among all of us children, my grandmother always had her favorite. Once, it was my older brother, Roberto, until she grew tired of him and sent him home. She took my brother, Criso, and threatened him with a syringe, telling him she would give him a shot if he did not behave. When she took my older sister,

Yayin, to the market, she pointed to a homeless drunk and told her that was her father. My sister came home crying and never wanted to go back.

Once, when I was walking with my mother, grandmother and Aunt Eneida, I was going to cross the street when she pulled me by my sleeve and pointed to a flat truck covered with a tarp that was coming. She told me that the truck was full of dead bodies being taken to the morgue, and if I didn't watch out I would be in that truck too, lost for eternity. Every time I see a flatbed truck now, it still gives me the shivers. I always recall her being a mean and wicked old lady. She did or said something mean and cruel like that to each one of us.

My Aunt Aminta could not have children. My grandmother wanted my mother and father to give our sister, Aminta Eneida, who we called Tita, to my Aunt Aminta. This aunt had tried endless times to have a baby, but at the third month she always miscarried, so she had stopped trying. My mother told grandmother that no matter how many children she had she was not about to give her child away. She was sorry that Aminta couldn't have children, but would not give away one of her own offspring.

My grandmother could not take no for an answer. So after four years she took matters into her own hands. When my Aunt Aminta came home for a visit, my grandmother took my sister, Tita, to spend time with her. We waited for her to come home to see what

Grandmother had said or done to her on that visit. We were not to see Tita again for many years.

Believing my grandmother when she said that my mother and father had signed all rights to their daughter for them to adopt her, Aunt Aminta had taken our sister to Spain. When my mother returned to bring her daughter home, she was gone. Aunt Aminta had just left that same day to go back to Spain. When our parents realized what our grandmother had done, they rushed to the airport to retrieve their daughter, but they arrived too late. My aunt and their daughter were gone. My grandmother had forged adoption papers and given Tita away. Now our sister was legally our Aunt Aminta's daughter. She grew up an only child thinking her family had given her away.

It wasn't enough that my grandmother had already taken over the raising of my mother's first-born, my older brother, Pibe. She took him as a child and raised him as her own. She prepared him to be a Catholic priest and sent him to Spain to further that goal. She sent him to a region relatively near Aunt Aminta, so she could be his guardian close by. When we were children, we were proud to say that our brother was studying to be a priest, again not understanding the circumstances. As an adult, I now know it was not in his heart to follow, but my grandmother's wishes to rule the lives of those around her, regardless of their feelings. The only consolation to my mother when Tita was taken away was that at least Pibe was living nearby in a boarding school. She hoped that he would be able to visit and try to keep close to Tita, so that neither of them would feel so alone. With both children thousands of miles away, she had no way to reach across to those two small children, to even reassure them of her love.

After much thought and regret, my mother wrote to her sister and explained what my grandmother had done. My mother and aunt came to an agreement. Since my aunt was so far away and did not know when she would return, they agreed that when my sister was old enough she should be told the truth about her family and what my grandmother had done. My sister's leaving left a void in our lives, especially my mother's. She cried for a long time, and she never again left any of us children alone with our grandmother.

In 1974 my grandmother died. Although I cried, I understood that my tears were not for her. They were for my mother, because I knew that she resented her own mother for what she had done, for what she was and the way she treated her. Our aunt never told our sister the whole truth. She grew up thinking her family had given her away. Today as an adult, our sister finally knows the real truth. And although she had more opportunities than her siblings, she grew up lonely in a "golden cage." She has her own resentments that she must forgive, forget or live with. She knows that no matter how far away we were from her, we all loved her unconditionally.

To my grandmother's family and friends who loved or cared for her, you may be disappointed—or even offended—to read of the bitter feelings we harbored against her. Perhaps she had a loving and kind heart for you, but she did not show that to me or my siblings. These words reflect the way our immediate family perceived her actions when we were children. If you have positive, caring memories of her, I'm grateful and respect the relationships you had. I only know the sorrow we all felt at the heartless intrusions that took two children away against our parents' wishes.

After the loss of our baby sister, Gloriela, and then the strange abduction of Tita, I was beginning to believe in the curse. I wondered if it really was going to follow us for the rest of our lives, to be passed on to all our children to come.

The Truck

CHAPTER 8

I come from a very large Latin family where many children are considered a blessing. It was not unusual to have ten or more children in one family. Our father was no exception. In Columbia, South America, his birthplace, our father had been married twice before coming to live permanently in Panamá. He left eleven children behind in that country. One day, Francisco, one of my father's sons, now grown, came to live with us. Together, they decided to buy a truck, because my father could no longer work on the farm and he needed a different way to provide for his family.

In the property between Achiote and the llanos, the dense woods helped my father decide to open a sawmill business. He thought that he and Francisco could sell the wood and transport it in the truck to the customers. We all helped to cut down the trees with a huge long saw. With a man on each side pushing and pulling, with sweat pouring off their brows, they worked sawing. They brought the logs into the village to a local sawmill, where they had a machine cut the trees into planks. A generator powered this machine. After they had invested some time and much labor in the cutting and transporting wood, a large company came into the village and bought out most of the woods from all of the surrounding region. My father had to give up yet another livelihood.

Father was then hired to build a cantina next to the lot neighboring our house. The truck still served a purpose. It had a crank in the front which we had to turn to start. We needed to be very careful, because sometimes it kicked back and knocked us on our butts, or it might kick our foreheads. Needless to say, the children were not supposed to touch it. The children went with some hired help to the farm and picked the coffee, fruit and vegetables, and then my father and Francisco used the truck to transport our goods to market.

We also used the truck to go to the beach about two hours away at a town called Piña. This beach is part of the Caribbean Sea, which is an arm of the Atlantic Ocean. We traveled there to get sand to add to the cement and gravel to make into blocks, which he then used to build the cantina. At the beach while we waited for my older brothers to load the sand into the truck, we younger children swam or played by the water's edge. The sand was beautifully white and we always enjoyed swimming and looking for sea shells.

During one of these trips to the beach, my little brother, Ramón, was left behind. We had traveled about fifteen minutes before we noticed he was missing. We had to turn around to go find him. My little brother was running, trying to catch up with us. He was very pale and sweaty. I will never forget his frightened and sad expression, and then the gladness and joy as he saw the truck coming back for him. My mother thought he was in the back with us; we thought he was in front with her, because we always took turns riding in front. From that day on we all teased our mother, telling her that if she didn't have so many children she wouldn't lose track of us.

That same evening this little brother almost lost his life. He and I were playing inside the back of the truck parked next to the cantina. He bent over to sit inside a spare tire that was leaning against the wall. The tire fell on him and his head became pinned inside the rim. It was raining so hard and I was yelling for anyone to help me move the tire off him. He was bleeding and I didn't know what to do except jump up and down, screaming hysterically to get someone's attention. I couldn't get down because the truck was too high. Finally, my father heard me screaming. When he got to my brother, he was almost unconscious and in a pool of blood. Mother took him and wrapped his head in a bed sheet. Without wasting a moment, Mother, Father and Francisco got in the truck and headed for Colón, to the same hospital that had saved my father's life.

We children were left in terror, waiting and waiting until our parents came home. Would they come with or without our little brother? Late that same night they returned home with my little brother, a bandage wrapped firmly around his head. To this day when he gets a very short hair cut you can see the V shaped scar on his head above the left ear. We can almost count the 107 stitches left there by that tire wound. It was a reminder for him and all of us that one minute you could be playing happily, and then the next, life can be ripped from you in the blink of an eye.

In this truck we also took a trip to the interior of the country and visited a different kind of beach. This beach had salt piles placed all over its expanse. We saw other trucks being loaded with it. Our father told us that the salt was being taken to the refineries to be sifted and cleaned so it would be edible and that this was the same kind of salt that we bought at the store. Salt sold in Panamá is very coarse and grainy. Until that day I never knew my country produced salt.

This same old truck transported our father and Francisco to Colombia to visit his other children. In my young imagination I was scared and didn't want my father to go. I imagined them crossing the Bridge of the Americas, taking them far away from us. I feared that our father would stay with his other family and never come back to us. The Americas' Bridge is the most expansive bridge in Panamá, dividing one side of the country from the other. I thought that after you crossed that bridge you could never come back. But although it seemed an eternity, they did return. I was happy to have my father home again.

The Cantina

B y this time we were living in the smaller house while my father settled in town and worked there finishing building and managing the cantina. This cantina was a bar, restaurant, and lodgings, not just for travelers but for anyone that partied too much and could not find his or her way home. Our father did not want any drunkards falling off a horse on his account. This building was a long ranch-style building made of cement. There were six bedrooms with a working bathroom, a kitchen with a propane stove, and, of course, a bar with a refrigerator.

The cantina had a generator that was turned on each afternoon, providing electricity and water to the building. Behind the cantina was a bathroom with running water. Next to the cantina Father also built a structure to house a coffee shucking machine. This building we called "the plant." Another generator provided electricity to run the machine. This machine looked very complicated to me; it resembled an enormous funnel. The coffee was fed into the mechanism and traveled through the plumbing until it came out clean into a massive barrel. From there it was packed in burlap bags. Another tube took the shells outside into the yard, where they were be piled up like warm mulch.

This cantina also served as a gathering place for the town's people. On the days that coffee was being shucked, the generator hummed all day. The refrigerator made ice and also kept water, sodas and beer cold for when the men finished their work. After a hard day's work the men came in for a cold drink. On the days that no coffee shucking was done, the people still came in the early afternoon and just hung around to talk. By four o'clock my father turned on the generator and music blared from a juke box where you deposited coins and the record magically came on. Then, the dancing started.

My father was always trying to make extra money close to home, so one year he tried growing rice. We had to plant a lot of the seed grain to yield enough rice. For us it was not economically feasible to grow this grain. Rice is grown in two ways, in dry land or wet land. We grew dry land rice. We harvested rice by hand so it took a long time. After picking the grain the outer yellow shell had to be removed. To accomplish this we used a pylon, which is made by hollowing out the top of a long piece of wood to resemble a tall bowl. With a drop hammer, also made of wood, we would pound and turn, pound and turn, until the shell was pulled away from the grain. After this was done, the rice was placed in a flat round tray. Again and again, we flipped it in the air, so that the shells blew in the wind, leaving the clean rice in the tray. But because un-shelled rice is cheaper, most of the village people purchased rice this way and shelled their own.

When the cantina and the failed rice-growing effort no longer generated enough income to support his growing family, Father was forced to find work outside our village. The only work he could find at the time was on a fishing boat, which took him out to sea—and away from us. Very far away from us.

.

Visiting Yayin

Our sister, Yayin, then married, moved away to another town called Salud. When we were out of school we went to spend time with her. She lived in a "family villa." The first time I visited her there I went on the truck her husband drove for a living. We drove past the village of Chagres. When we got to the town of Palmas Bellas, we had to cross the lake to get to the other side. It did not have a bridge and I wondered how in the world we were supposed to get to the other side. All of the passengers got out and my brother-in-law told me to stay in the truck. I noticed we were driving right into the lake onto a barge that took us across. I was fearful that the whole bus would fall into the lake. I was the only human passenger inside the truck full of produce, but we crossed without incident. After the successful crossing, I realized it was kind of fun being the only one in the bus crossing the lake. The passengers had to wait for the bus to cross so the barge could come back and pick them up. After a few trips they were all back on the truck and we were on our way again.

Going from Chagres to Salud, the houses seemed to huddle more closely together. It was more of a small city than a town. There were more stores and businesses than in our small village. Most of them had electricity. The terrain was laced with valleys and mountains, not so much jungle. It was more open and you could see for miles from that elevation in the mountains. I saw flowers of all colors, like a rainbow, as we drove down the road.

I was happy to see my sister. The land of the "family villa," where she lived, was owned by her in-laws. All the family members had their homes there. It was their own community, which consisted of the main house where the parents lived, and smaller family homes, one for each married family member.

In the bottom of the clearing between Yayin's house and the main house was a well where we fetched water and went every morning to bathe and wash clothes. They had cemented the inside walls of the well and the outside surrounding the clearing, so when you went there you would not get muddy. When I stayed with her, Yayin always sent me to Bible school with the other children. I loved going to Bible school, so I could learn more about God and Jesus. The nuns read us stories and we played games or drew pictures, but whatever we did, I always enjoyed it. After Bible school we walked back home for lunchtime and then had the rest of the afternoon to play.

The main house had a generator that they turned on

every afternoon after dinner to bring running water from the well into the house. When the generator was turned on, the bathroom had running water, as did the kitchen, for doing the dishes. After the dishes were done we could watch television. Usually we watched the news. Then my favorite show, *Bonanza*, came on. I fell in love with Little Joe and told myself that if ever I found the right man and had a son, his name would be Michael, like Michael Landon.

My sister also sent me to see the nuns, who had a clinic a few miles down the road. They treated minor injuries, but mainly they handed out vitamins to the children. Yayin always gave me money to take the bus back to her house, but I liked to walk and see all of the interesting sights that contrasted with my home. I liked to stop along the way to eat from the fruit trees that lined the road. There is a tree which yields a purple grapefruit-sized fruit called "mamey," and it is extraordinarily sweet. I stopped to enjoy this fruit without having to share it with anyone, which did not happen very often. Along the road were also lush mango and orange trees. Mamey was my favorite fruit, because we did not grow that in my village.

Sometimes, we went hunting for land crabs. During this time it was mating season, and crabs were widespread throughout the villa. They were easy to catch. We made hooks with a wire hanger and picked them up, then dropped them into a bucket fast, so they wouldn't pinch us with their claws. After we had a few buckets filled, we made an open fire outside and put the clean crabs in an incredibly large pot. When they were cooked, we shared a feast.

During Easter the women gathered in the morning to make food for the entire day. We celebrated Easter by having a procession and praying. During the procession the Virgin Mary was carried throughout the town. We sang and prayed until we returned her to her place in the church. The women made foods I had never eaten before. They made "Chocao" from ripe plantains. Until that day I had eaten plantains fried or in soups, but not like this. They cooked them with milk and sugar and made a pudding. We had rice with raisins, as well as different dishes made out of yucca. We also drank a variety of "chichas," which are refreshments made from fruits or vegetables.

And like every country in the world, we savor eating—both for the tasty nutrition, but also for the warmth and companionship as we gather around the food. I always enjoyed going to visit with my sister Yayin.

Magistrate

While my father was at sea, even though he sent money home, my mother found a job to help with the expenses. She was hired as Magistrate to take care and keep the law in our town. She was happy that she did not have to leave town to find work. She learned the rules of law so that she could do this job efficiently. When my mother assumed this responsibility, it meant she presided over the town in an important way. She had one policeman to help her maintain law and order. This also meant that her family had to set an example for everyone else and not shame or embarrass her.

After my father returned home from sea and my mother was established in her job, she hired him and other men in town to build a jail, which also served as her office. Then she had a two-story school house, a Catholic Church and a community water pump next to the school built. Now we also had better roads. She had these building built in the middle of town, so families living at opposite ends of town walked about the same distance to all the facilities. Sometimes, when the jungle was engulfing the road, she would have the prisoners along with the men in town go to cut and burn down the encroaching arms of the jungle.

This was an alternative way for the prisoners to pay their fines, if they didn't have money. Usually, she had them do community service, or work for the family they had wronged. Most of the criminals in her jail were village people being held for misdemeanors. If anyone committed a major crime she sent them to the city, and the authorities then handled those cases there.

While the men were working the women would make a big pot of "sancocho," which is like a thick soup, to feed them all. Our mother followed all the rules without exception. Once, she even put our father in jail along with some other men who were drunk and disorderly. We all wanted to know why she had put our father in jail. Her response was, "He broke the law. I have to follow the rules. If I don't punish him along with the others I will lose respect or even my job." I didn't know what that meant then. Never again did my father break the law. From then on he was a model example to the whole village.

While our mother worked, we girls were in charge of keeping house, making lunches, and having dinner ready by the time she returned. At noon our mother came home for lunch and siesta. Siesta starts at 12:00 noon. This is a rest period, because the sun is so hot during this time. In most Hispanic countries, people take a siesta and all business is closed. They return to work at 2:00PM and stay open again until 9:00PM. When she had meetings or was really busy, she sent a child from that side of town with a message to bring her lunch. On those days she skipped the siesta and stayed indoors.

Before our mother left for work she told us to play "Pretend." My older brother, Roberto, would be the "father" and he would take his "sons," Criso and Ramón, hunting or fishing, while as the oldest girl I would be the "mommy," teaching the "daughters," Cecilia and Maity, to cook, clean and do laundry. This is how my mother taught us household responsibilities. When she returned from work, she expected the house to be clean, the dishes to be washed and the laundry to be hanging on the line. After that was done we had time to play, and we took full advantage of playtime. We went to the plant to see what was going on there, play with the other children or just hang out. Sometimes in our mother's absence, we got away with things she had told us not to do.

Along the side of our small house, a stream ran slowly under the road. Nearby, there was a massive tubing where I used to hide when we played hide-and-seek at night. Because it was full of bats no one ever looked there and I never got caught. This stream seemed to come from high above in the mountain, almost from out of the rocks.

One day while our mother was working, my

brothers, Roberto and Criso, and some friends decided to find the source of this stream. I decided to tag along. Our mother often warned us not to climb that mountain because of the dangers lurking about. We thought she would not find out. We should have known better, since she always said she had eyes in the back of her head. We had climbed about a mile with no sign of the source of this stream. We were crossing the rocks on top of the waterfall. The rocks were slippery from mold and running water; I stepped on a slippery rock and my feet flew from under me. I was sliding down the jagged rocks when my hand frantically grasped some vines clinging to the growth at the edge of the waterfall. All of the kids started to pull on the vine to help me up until they could reach my arm. I was lucky, because if I had plummeted to the bottom, I am sure that the rocks would have cut through me like a knife. We were all very frightened. I knew that they had saved me from an imminent death. We turned around and went back home before something worse happened.

Upset that I had tagged along and ruined their adventure, my brothers chided that girls should just stay home and not follow men. That time we didn't find the source of the stream. On the way along the stream we did find "posos," pools of water near the bank. They seemed to come right out of the rocks forming small pockets of water where only one or two people could get in. The water was so inviting, clear and cool that we could just sit there for hours, enjoying the coolness on a hot summer day. Even though we went inside these "posos," we had to be extremely careful. Some of them were incredibly deep and a wrong move could cause a drowning.

The surrounding floor of these landings was covered with green moss, like an exceptionally soft carpet under our bare feet. Fruit trees were all around us, laden with ripe fruit. We filled our bellies with it as we enjoyed the swim, and then hit each other with the pits of the fruit. As children in this paradise, we enjoyed life and didn't have a care in the world. People said that these water pools had healing powers and were a fountain of youth. We thought that maybe we could stay there forever and not grow old. To this day my sisters and I wonder why this "miracle water of youth" did not affect any of us. We still grew older.

Years later my younger sister, Cecilia, related to me how they had found the source of the stream. It was a large lagoon miles above on the mountain. Rain filled this lagoon and it overflowed, making the waterfall, which in turn carried the water down to smaller lagoons and into the little stream beside our house.

The Radio

For as long as I can remember, my father had a small, hand-held, battery-operated radio. This radio was our primary source of information from the outside world. My father woke up about 5:00 every morning. He immediately turned on the radio. It was very loud, because this was our wake-up call. As my father made coffee, all the children stayed in bed and listened to the dueling banjos, followed by Mexican music, and then a program called "Escuelita Para Todos"—School for Everyone. This was a fifteen-minute, fact-oriented, educational program. Each morning there was a focus on a different country, followed by the news. Then, the radio was turned off.

My father went to work; my mother got up and made breakfast. Around 7:00AM my father returned to eat. We knew that by then we all had better be up and ready to start the day. At noon and six in the afternoon the radio was turned on again to hear the news of the day. On Wednesdays and Sundays at noon, right before the news, we gathered and listened to the lottery.

The radio station we listened to was in Colón, because sometimes they broadcast a message to someone in the village. We received both good messages and not-so-good messages. I remember the morning that we got a very bad message. It was for the family of 'John Doe' and the message was from the hospital. "ATTENTION FAMILY: 'JOHN DOE' IN THE VILLAGE OF ACHIOTE, YOUR SON 'W. DOE' PASSED AWAY LAST NIGHT." And they repeated the communication several times during the day, so that the family was certain to hear it.

This particular young man had been hunting a few weeks before. He had stepped on a rusty nail but did not take care of it. When several days had passed and he could hardly walk, his foot became discolored and swollen. His family took him to the hospital, but because they could not afford to stay in the city, they left him there and returned home to attend to their crops. Every day, they had news from the hospital through the radio. They found out that their son had contracted gangrene; that it had made its way into his blood; and finally, that it had poisoned him and taken his life. We were on our way to school and my sister, Yayin, told us children not to tell the family, because she was older and knew how to tell them better than we might. By the time she reached their house, the family was crying and we knew that they had gotten the bad news. Now, they had to go to the city and collect his body for burial.

I also remember my mother coming home early from work one day. It appeared that she had been crying. Of course, we were curious as to why my mother would be crying, and wondered if she had received bad news. We urged her to tell us what she was crying about. She said it was very bad news, that she had heard the news on the radio that the American President John F. Kennedy had been assassinated. After explaining to us what "assassinated" meant, she also informed us that this was tragic news for many people all over the world. At the time I did not understand why my mother would cry for a person she didn't even know in a far away land.

It was not until years later as an adult that I understood the importance of the radio. I felt the full impact of that medium of communication when my sister, Yayin, announced our father's funeral date for everyone to hear, so they could attend if they wished.

CHAPTER 13

The Flood

Panamá has two seasons: one is the dry season and the other is rainy. Severe tropical rains and treacherous slopes with rock very near the surface can create dangerous flood conditions quickly with little warning, especially around the Chagres River.

During one season of rain six of us children almost lost our lives to a flood. My parents had gone to the city, leaving us alone. My older brother, Roberto, was left in charge, as Yayin had gotten married and moved away. And of course, we had neighbors nearby who always kept a watchful eye. Usually, my mother announced to the neighbors that she was going to the city and asked them to keep an eye on us and to report to her if we misbehaved.

It started to rain in the late afternoon, so we used our indoor time to prepare our breakfast for the next morning. It is easier to fry elephant ears if you make them at night, let them rise overnight and fry them in the morning. After putting all the chairs on top of the table and bringing the food to the upstairs kitchen, we settled down for the night with no foreboding of disaster. Sometimes, when it flooded the water would be downstairs, but we would still be dry upstairs, so we were not worried. In the morning Roberto woke us up, because the water had reached to the second floor and to our beds. After raining all night the river had overflowed, inundating our house with inconceivable volumes of water.

From our upstairs porch to the road we had a wooden plank which we kept on the porch for just this kind of emergency. The idea was that we could walk across it if circumstances like these ever presented themselves. But this time the plank was waving in the water and it was impossible to walk across it. We thought it would be best to hold on to it as we swam across, keeping the plank between us and the river's current as we worked our way to the road.

My three smallest siblings, Ramón, Cecilia and Maity, could not swim, so each of the older children, Roberto, Criso and I, carried them on our backs holding onto them with one hand and to the plank with the other as we swam to safety. Roberto decided that Criso would carry Ramón, I would carry Maity, and he would carry Cecilia because he was the oldest and Cecilia was always afraid of everything. Swimming across was very difficult, not only because we had to swim against the current, but because the current from the river behind our house was strong. We all knew that if we lost hold of the plank before reaching the road, the current could sweep us all out into the river and to our death.

I could see Roberto struggling to keep Cecilia above water because all of the insects in the water had her more scared than the flood. Ramón and Maity were not as frightened, but they did know that if they didn't help behave and hang onto the plank, it would be harder to get to the road. As we swam to safety we saw our possessions, including our breakfast, flooding away in the water along with water snakes, spiders and other animals and insects swimming for safety just like the six of us, working hard to get to high ground. We worked our way to the road, swam right over the hibiscus fence and onto the hill across from our house, where an empty house awaited us.

This house belonged to friends of the family who were still in their home in the mountains. We took shelter there and waited and prayed that our parents would look for us, and find us. We knew that these people would be happy to have helped us even when they were not home. This house was like most any other house in our town; it was open with only four posts and a thatch roof. They had no beds but did have one big hammock in the middle of the room, which all six of us crawled into, happy and scared at the same time—happy because we were all together and safe in one piece, scared because the whole town was under water. We had no idea what had been the fate of the other people in town. And, our mother and father were not there to reassure us.

At night when I could not sleep I heard the rain. It did not sound like our zinc roof when I imagined something was frying on a hot pan. Lying there awake I also wondered where my parents were and if they were safe, not knowing if they would find us.

In the early morning we heard loud noises and ran outside to see what it was. The United States Army, which had a training base close to our town, came in helicopters and dropped food and clothing to the flood victims. They dropped cans full of cheese and crackers that opened with a tab on the lid. We ate that because at this house the people had not left food. It was their practice to take it with them when they went to their other house in the mountains. The food drop of rations came like manna from heaven, so it relieved our worry about going hungry. My family and the whole town were very grateful for that food and clothing, that evidence of human care across boundaries.

Three days went by, and still there was no sign of our parents. Late that third night we heard my mother's sweet voice calling for us. She had worked her way into town in a canoe and was frantically looking for us, fearing that all six of her children might have drowned. She said that she had tried to rent a canoe to bring her into town, but that no one would risk their lives coming here. Finally, after the rain stopped and the waters began to subside she saw a friend coming this way who brought her.

When the flood dried up and the town was visible again, we all counted our losses. They were very numerous. We lost most of our animals; everything inside the house was gone; and the house was no longer sturdy. We lived in that house for a while longer, but cautiously. Then a few months later we built a smaller house a little ways down the road from our two-story house that had been home. I loved that house, and I never understood why we did not rebuild it.

Some people say that bad things come in threes; for us it was in fours. I don't know if I believe it, but I do know that in a very short time we lost our farm, our possessions and our two-story home. Most important of all, my father lost his health, Tita was gone, and we lost our baby sister, Gloriela. Again, I wondered about that dark curse. Was it really going to follow us for the rest of our lives and be passed on to all our children to come?

School and the
American Soldiers

Our school was a two-story building staffed with four teachers. The downstairs was open and it served as a classroom. When I first started school, one side of that downstairs was for kindergarten and first grade; the other half was for second and third grades. Upstairs were two rooms, one for fourth and fifth grades and the other room for sixth grade.

Since the downstairs was open we could see everything that went on around us. Just outside near the road was the community water pump for those on that side of town who were too far from "our stream." From our classroom we could see and hear people pumping their water and gathering to catch up on each others' lives. Their gossip and laughter often distracted us from our school work. It was also a comforting connection to our community.

I had a female teacher who was very abusive—not just to me but to everyone. As soon as girls are born in our culture we have our ears pierced. When I was learning to read and I could not read fast enough for this teacher's liking, she pulled at my ears by the ear-rings and twisted them. She also had the bad habit of slapping our open hands with the ruler when we mis-behaved. Sometimes, she even turned our hands over and hit our knuckles with this ruler.

As my luck would have it, one of the other teachers left, and this teacher took over the duties of the next two grades. Now our classes became split into kinder-garten, first and second in the bottom part of the school. In the other two rooms upstairs were third and fourth and then fifth and sixth in the next room. And so, for four long years my life was pure torture. All my love of school became filled with hate for this one woman, as she ruined my early learning years.

Almost by defiance I learned to read, just to show her that I could. I wanted to be in the fifth grade more than anything, because then I would get away from her.

When I was in the fourth grade all of us children from the village were taken by the American soldiers in a United States Army truck on a trip to a nearby city called Chagres, which had a medical facility. We each received a shot on the upper arm for polio. I had never had a shot before and it was very painful. All of us children cried on the trip home.

In all the small villages we were considered poor and malnourished, so once a week the students were given two vitamin pills provided by the government. To this day I can smell and taste those awful pills; they looked small and were yellow and brown like M & Ms but not at all sweet. As the saying goes, "It was a hard pill to swallow," and most of the children would be vomiting by the end of the day.

The government also provided milk. The most responsible fifth or sixth grade girl got to pick a partner and go downstairs where she built an open fire to cook the milk—water and powdered milk was mixed. We stirred until it boiled but had to take care not to burn the milk or let it boil over. Afterwards, we lined up all of the kids and gave them each a glass. This was done once a week. At the end of the month if we had milk left over, we made enough to have two glasses each. On milk days we had to bring our own cup with us. When I reached fifth grade, most of the time I was chosen for this job, and I felt very grown up.

Being "grown up," I was sent by my mother to stay with a friend of hers who owned one of the stores in town. Her husband had died suddenly and she was all alone. Although she was older than my mother, she had no children. So to ease the loss of her husband, my mother asked me to help her with the store, and to stay with her at night. This friend was afraid to sleep alone, because she thought that her dead husband would come back and take her with him. I was scared that he would come back and pull my leg, but I also felt proud to be there, helping her. I knew I was doing something good. While I stayed with her she gave me cookies to take to school and share with my brothers and sisters. I stayed with her for two weeks until she felt she could cope by herself.

When I returned to my village as an adult I visited this lady. She looked so old, but she still remembered that it was Carmencita that had stayed with her in her time of need.

When I was young I was very afraid of the American soldiers, because when we went to the city, they used to stop our bus and search it. I never knew why or what they were looking for, but I was always intimidated and scared when they boarded our bus. They carried rifles and their imposing stature dwarfed our small size.

That changed when one year they came to school and took us on a truck ride to the Fort Davis American Army base near the city of Colón. There they treated us to lunch, and they gave us each a number which we redeemed for a toy. On the way there and back they tried to talk to us and make us laugh. They didn't seem so menacing now, and we were always glad to receive a toy. Toys were not something we got often. I remember being given a doll when I was young. My sisters and I shared the doll and played together with it for endless hours.

I also remember my mother telling us about the soldiers who came to the hospital to give blood to my little sister, Cecilia, when she had severe anemia. At this time my older sister, Judy, was married to a soldier and they lived in the city. They heard of my little sister needing blood and that our father couldn't pay for it. In Panamá blood is not free. Our brother-in-law, Martin, got a lot of his soldier friends together to help. They came to the hospital and donated the blood to save Cecilia's life. To this day we are all grateful to him and his friends for that gift of life they freely gave to our sister. And we tease her telling her she has gringo blood. The soldiers and their gifts definitely made our Christmas much more fun. At the time I really didn't appreciate the American soldiers. I just knew I was afraid of them. Now I know how much they do for the world. America's freedom depends on them. They are brave men and women, who try to keep peace and order in this world.

The Canal

I n Panamá, every year at the end of January and the first part of February we celebrate Carnival. The whole country is crowded with people from all over the world. This time is the most beautiful and colorful time of the year for those who work all year on their elaborate costumes and floats. They have a large procession, with singing and dancing in the streets. This is a traditional and somewhat religious celebration. Us,ually there is a Mass before any festivities begin. Unlike here in the U.S., where the Mardi Gras is only in the city of New Orleans, ours is in every city in the country that can afford the kind of money that is spent on these celebrations.

During Carnival, our parents took us to the City of Colón to watch the parade of floats with all the elaborate costumes and festive decorations. They thought it was important for us to participate in this important cultural event. Although we could not afford costumes, my mother purchased the always popular fish net stockings and painted our faccs with layers of colorful make-up. This was the only time we were allowed to wear make-up. Stockings were different colors for each girl; the boys were given a devil's whip or some sort of hat, depending on what the small savings would allow. No matter what we got, we always had fun just being part of the crowd and watching the entire goings-on in the street.

Since we went to the city in the truck, we took pillows and blankets. When the children got tired, Mother would just lay us down in the back of the truck while the adults continued partying close by.

On our way to the city of Colón, we had to cross the Gatun locks. This is one of the three locks that comprise the Panamá Canal. At night as we approached the locks, when the ships were lined up waiting to cross, the lights cast beautiful beams across the water. It looked like they were Christmas trees resting on their sides as they slowly made their way through the locks. The ships were aglow not only with lights, but with flags from all over the world.

The country of Panamá is very small—about the size of West Virginia—with close to three million inhabitants. The north borders with Costa Rica, and the south with Colombia.

In the late 1850s a railroad was built by the French to aid travelers trekking through the dense jungles of Panamá. They were generally migrating from east to west during the California gold rush.

In 1882 the French purchased the rights to build a

canal across the center of Panamá to save a great amount of time and resources for the ships coming north from the Atlantic or south to the Pacific and on to California. They all had to travel around the Cape Horn of Argentina in South America. Building the canal through Panamá would save them 17,000 miles of travel.

I watched the ships slowly making their way through the three seats of Gatun locks. When a ship enters the canal, the captain relinquishes his command to the canal captain. This captain is trained in navigating these waters. A canal captain must undergo years of training to be able to qualify to take ships through the canals, because of low water levels, sand, and sometimes even mudslides. If you did not know your way through these waters, you could sand barge the ship, in which case it would be there for days, losing travel time and money, and possibly obstructing the passage of others.

I saw the tug boat come along the ship to pull it far enough to reach the mules, which are crane-like machines that drag the ship through the three sets of locks by heavy ropes. As the ships came closer to the first set of locks, water poured to flood the first set, lowered to the second set, and then raised again to the third, bringing water to the level of the lake, and finally onto the other side of the lake, where the tug boat was waiting to help the ship onto the ocean. As I watched, I could read the names of the vessels. Big and bright, one read "Del Monte," and it made me hungry.

The Frenchman, Steven DeLasept, had built the Suez Canal in Egypt, and he was positive he could build the canal in Panamá. For years, he worked hard and lost many men to the alternating torrents of tropical rains, mudslides, yellow fever and malaria. Finally, he gave up the fight, and France sold the canal-building rights to the United States.

The Americans did not want to work on a country that belonged to another, so they helped the Panamanians fight for freedom against Colombia. In 1903 Panamá gained freedom and has been free ever since.

The French had the idea to dig a ditch all the way across Panamá, but nature just did not cooperate with them. The Americans did what the French had rejected. That was to dam the Chagres River and create a high-level lake. They adopted a plan that engineered giant locks as a kind of water stairway to move ships up and down from the lake. It took four years to create this waterway called Gatun Lake. At that time, Gatun was the largest man-made lake in the world.

The waterway that constitutes the Panamá Canal is fifty miles long from the Atlantic to the Pacific Ocean and is ten miles wide. There are three sets of different locks from Panamá City on the Pacific side to the City of Colón on the Atlantic side. These include the Pedro

Miquel and Miraflores, which have one set of locks, and Gatun, which has three sets of locks. It takes one ship roughly seven to thirteen hours to make the passage through the locks. When a ship's captain makes a reservation, it is given priority. Each ship is charged a toll, based on ton weight, to go through the locks. According to the records, the highest toll ever paid was $107,000 by the Queen Elizabeth II. In contrast, the smallest toll was .36 cents and was paid in 1928 by an American who was permitted to swim across the canal. In order to cross the canal, ships have to be raised and then lowered to move from one level of the ocean to another.

The wait to cross the locks was sometimes hours, although there were times when the workers closed the locks, so the cars could cross and they could continue their work. When the locks are closed, it makes a bridge. It seemed to me that crossing this bridge was dangerous because it's terribly narrow. If a car made a wrong move it would fall into the water. But to this day, I have heard of only one car plummeting into the water, and that was a drunk driver who drove right off the bridge.

I liked to wait and watch the ships go up and down, and then on to the lake, on their way to the ocean beyond. It gave me a tremendous amount of pride to see the ships move through, because my father had worked here when he was very young. The Panamá Canal is said to be one of the Seven Wonders of the

World. It was built at a time when technology was considered inferior by today's standards. With only minimal repairs, the canal still functions with all of the original components it had in the early 1900s. The only exception is that the waterways were widened from seven to ten miles to accommodate bigger and more modern ships. And now, engineers all over the world are looking into some kind of improvement to accommodate even larger ships. The canal has been operating since 1914 and has never been closed due to repairs.

The Americans were in charge of the canal until 1999, when it was handed over to the Panamanian government. On the front lines we have very well trained and capable Panamanians who know what they are doing. Some of them started as janitors, later went to school for better training, and now play key roles in the proper running of the canal.

* Information from: *Commemorative Album of 75th Anniversary, 1914-1989*

The City

The city of Panamá was very different from my little village. It was crowded with people and traffic; I had never seen so many cars in my life. The sidewalks were swarming with vendors. It was an open market where we could purchase everything we needed. I did not go to the city often. My mother went alone or only took one of us with her. Each week she took a different child, going to the city on the weekend to purchase staple foods. There were tall buildings with apartments where people were jam-packed.

When I graduated from sixth grade my Aunt Aminta, who was living in Panamá City, now took me to live with her so that I could continue my education. She, her husband, and my sister, Tita, had come back to Panamá after a long stay overseas. I was excited to go live with my sister, because we would have the chance to get to know each other. I was also very scared, because I had only been in Panamá City a few times to visit relatives. To me it was a very overpowering city.

The school was also enormous compared to my little village. The school was only for kids in the 7th grade and it had three floors. There were about 900 students in that grade. Every Monday morning we gathered in the courtyard and pledged allegiance to the flag, sang the National Anthem and said a prayer, before our day began. The grade system started from 7-A and it went to 7-Z, and your grade average determined your assigned homeroom. My average was low so my homeroom was 7-N.

I felt lost, left out and out of place. It was that way through the whole school year. During conferences the parents of my homeroom gathered together. The teacher called out each child's name, and the parents raised their hands. She then announced to everyone in the room all the grades and behavior of the child. When my aunt returned home, she told me the humiliation and embarrassment I had caused her by both bad grades and my behavior. I prayed to get to the ninth grade, so that I could quit and go someplace else.

In Panamá when you graduate from ninth grade you have the option of staying in school until twelfth grade and going on to college or going to trade school. In trade school you work as you learn and do not "waste" time going to school learning useless facts— so I thought. I also missed my family and my village. At school I was sure that my English teacher was against me. She was not a likable person. Again and again, she told me I was stupid, that I had a face like a horse and that I would never learn anything. I already hated school from my grade school years. I didn't think this was worth it. I even thought about telling my aunt to send me home where I belonged, but I didn't want to shame my family, so I stuck it out.

One time when the teacher was on her normal rampage towards me, she told me to get up. Getting up and standing for the rest of the class time was the equivalent of being in the corner or having a dunce's hat. I was spending most of my time standing, but this time I had done nothing to deserve punishment. I was amazed when all the other students also got up and told the teacher that she had no reason to treat me that way. They would not sit until she stopped. After that incident, this teacher left me alone. She wasn't nice to me, but she didn't harass me either. It was like I didn't exist to her. I did not mind.

With so many children in this school, we had two shifts. I went in the afternoon from 12:30 to 4:00. After school I was to get on the city bus to go home. It cost 10 cents. My aunt always gave me 25 cents so that I could have enough to pay the bus fare and also buy a snack. After school one day, I could not find my 25 cents; I knew that someone had taken it. I remembered lending a pencil to a girl and she went into my book bag to get it. Although I did not accuse her, I knew that she had to have taken it because I had never lost my money before. While on the bus not finding my money, I started to cry and the lady next to me asked me why I was crying. I told her I had lost my money and couldn't pay my fare. She told me not to cry that she would pay. I was so happy.

The next time I could not find my money, I had to walk home. I didn't know how to get home so I followed the route the bus took. I knew it would take me a long time to get home and I'd better walk fast, but I couldn't help looking at what went on as I walked. I passed the "Casa Blanca," which is comparable to the White House. I passed through Santana Park where the lottery is drawn twice a week. I also passed the ice house, where the trucks or people bought ice by the block. When I came to the University of Panamá, I knew I was half way home. I was so tired.

It was about 7:00PM when I was on the last hill before the house and almost home, when my aunt and uncle came up on me. Upset and worried that I had not arrived, she demanded to know what I was doing since 4:00. I told her I had lost my bus fare and had to walk home. She wanted to know why I had not called her so she could come get me. She said that something bad could have happened to me and she would not have known. I told her that I didn't know how to use the phone. We never had a phone at home, so I was not ever taught how to use one. I felt very ignorant at that moment, but so happy that at last I made it home safe and sound. I learned my lesson about never letting anyone look in my book bag. That night my aunt showed me how to use the phone. In light of my adventures that day, she even carefully instructed me in how to make a collect call.

In the middle of the school year my aunt informed Tita and I that we would be moving to Fort Davis. I was ecstatic because I would be close to my family and could see them more often. My aunt enrolled me in a smaller school. This one had only two floors, and it was seventh through twelve grades. Fort Davis was an American base and everyone spoke English. Even though my sister tried to teach me at that time, I didn't think I would ever need it, and I was not willing to learn. Again I felt left out. Since I was close to the Gatun locks, it was my habit to go for a walk and on a hill close to the locks, as close to the water as possible, I often sat. Watching the ships going to far away lands, I wished I were in one of them also going to a far away land. Little did I know that soon I would be leaving my homeland far behind and traveling to a foreign country.

"Be careful what you wish for; it may come true." Not so long after that I was told I would be going to the United States. And my life was forever changed. When I landed in Miami some friends of my aunt met me. They lived in Hollywood, Florida; I thought it was so cool to be in Hollywood. I did not know that it was not the Hollywood of the movies. I was surprised that the people here did not wear military uniforms like they did on the base. I just figured that every American wore one.

Here the scenery was similar to Panamá's with a green, lush and beautiful landscape. We went sight-seeing to a shipyard. I don't really remember much of it, except that I loved seeing the ships. After three days they put me on a plane for Detroit to meet my sister and her family. I had not seen this sister for a long time. She had married and moved to the States with her soldier husband when I was a young child, so I did not get to see her often and didn't really know her well. Now, she and her husband had four boys. I was to live with them, so that I could have a better opportunity to improve my life and could help her with the children.

In December when I arrived in Detroit, it was dark and cold. To me it was the dead of winter. I was not accustomed to the cold weather. In the morning I saw snow for the first time in my life. Everything was frozen and dead. I didn't know what to think. After the Christmas holiday I was enrolled in the local school. Now, I was forced to learn English. And now, I was determined to prove my former teacher in Panamá wrong and my aunt, too. I would learn English—even better than her. And I did. At that time I was the only Hispanic in school, and they did not have translators as they do today. They did, however, have a Spanish class, and the teacher sometimes helped me.

Most of the time I spent my lunch hour with the English teacher, learning to read from the books called *Reading is Fundamental*, the books for kindergarten.

Because I loved to read I missed reading "real books" and I wanted to fit in. Having no distractions helped me to learn fast. Spring had come and I saw dead trees and flowers come to life almost like a miracle. That miracle encompassed me, too, because by the end of that school year I was on the same level as my classmates academically.

Illegal Alien

When I was in the tenth grade and still living in the United States, my sister and her whole family went to Panamá without me. I was disappointed, even devastated emotionally. I didn't know why I was not going with them to see my family. I missed them so much. My sister informed me that I could not return to Panamá, because if I did I wouldn't be able to come back. I didn't ask her any questions—I just didn't know what to ask. By then, I had started dating David, who is now my husband. I told him what my sister had said.

We decided to go see our high school principal. I told him about my sister going to Panamá without me and showed him my passport. After looking at it he said I was illegal and didn't hesitate to tell me that I had to go back to Panamá. He also said that since he was the principal he could not help me because of rules, but he would talk to the vice-principal and told me not to worry. He suggested that I could apply for a student visa and that all would work out.

In subsequent weeks David, his mother Mary, the

vice-principal and I made a few trips to the Immigration and Naturalization office in Detroit. I was very nervous, because I did not know what to expect. I went before a judge for a hearing. I was deported. The judge was favorably impressed that I had come forward, so he wrote a letter of recommendation to the American Consulate in Panamá to expedite a student visa. I returned home to Panamá.

I was so surprised when I got home. Now my family owned a house by the beach in a different village. Unlike the beaches we had visited when I was a child, this sand was green. I had never seen green sand before. It was different, but also beautiful. My mother had written often and told me they had sold the properties in our small town and now had this house. This house was very close to the beach and it was a ranch-style house made of cement. The roof was constructed of clay panels, because zinc would have been rusted by the sea salt.

When I looked out the window or sat on the porch my eyes scanned the ocean and the ships on the horizon, making their way to the locks. In the late afternoon the sunset was a most beautiful fire orange or sometimes mixed colors, like crimson. At night the full moon cast its light and reflected on the ripples of the water, dancing in the wind. When I was young, I thought that I lived in Paradise, but this was the real thing. Today when I need to, I close my eyes and see it all as if I were there.

Now that I was home, I saw my family differently, with the eyes of an unwilling outsider. They were close to one another, and I didn't seem to fit in. I didn't belong here anymore, yet I felt that I didn't belong in the States either. I was confused. I sat down in the sand, watching the waves hit the shore. I asked God for help, to give me a sign or some guidance about where I belonged. Two months later I was granted exchange student status and was given a visa for three years.

David and I graduated from high school in June, 1976. My visa would expire in two weeks and again I had to return to Panamá.

In August of that same year David came to Panamá. As soon as he got off the airplane we went to the magistrate. My mother, father, and an older sister were with us. Even though they wanted us to wait, they did not object. The judge asked some strangers to be our witnesses and I translated our vows to David. We were married and spent two weeks in this paradise. David always jokes and tells everyone that my father had a gun to his head and he had to get married.

The small town where we were married is called Portobelo, overlooking the Caribbean. This port town was a major trading route during the 1500s. The ruins here are almost identical to those found in St. Augustine, Florida, and in Puerto Rico. The Spaniards protected the city until Henry Morgan, the infamous pirate, plundered, burned and stole not only our country's gold, but all the riches of the small islands of the Caribbean.

Today, in Portobelo the "Cristo Negro" (Black Christ) celebration takes place every year on October 21st. People from all over the world come in pilgrimage to celebrate the feast of this patron saint. People pay their respects by wearing robes and some by crawling to the town or walking bare-footed for miles. Some of them bring "ofrendas," which are gifts of thanks for a miracle that was granted. They pin their ofrendas to the robe of the Christ figure. In fact, my parents offered such a gift for my brother and me when we had surgery.*

People say that all year long this stone figure is too heavy to move; the only time it can be done is during the procession. The procession starts around seven in the evening at the church, moves through the main street, and continues until they have walked through the entire town, finally reaching the church again. When the Christ is returned to the church, parties and celebrations begin, sometimes lasting for days.

I stayed in Panamá while I applied for residency in the United States. David had gone back to Bellevue, Michigan to start college. In November of 1976, I was granted residency status. I had to report to the govern-

* To read this story, look for:
The Courage to Live: My Journey with God.
A Kidney Patient's Story at www.acornpublishing.com

ment the first of every year by going to the post office and filling out an information form, so that I would not lose my green card.

Now, I wanted to apply for my citizenship. I could not initiate the process until I had been a legal resident in the United States for five years. The time I had spent here as a student did not count. While I waited and lived my life with David, I often studied a game called *Your America* and learned as much about the country and the workings of the government as I could. I wanted to pass the necessary test, so that I could help my family come to this country, as I had done.

During this time I also changed religions. I felt that the Catholic faith was not for me. I was not learning from it, and learning was always a priority for me. I switched to the Methodist faith, which had been the church in which David grew up.

In 1981 I passed the test. With many others from around the world, we raised our right hands and took the oath of citizenship. For me, after those intervening years, becoming an American citizen was a long-awaited milestone.

When I told my mother about becoming an American citizen, and also about changing religions, she was very angry. She told me I had renounced my country and my faith, and God was not happy with these choices. I was born Catholic and I should be buried Catholic. I tried to explain my reasons for the change, but she did not want to listen, let alone understand. It took her a very long time to accept my decisions. When she was upset with me for other reasons, she always brought this up. I had to ignore her when she tried to tell me that God was angry with me. I know that God loves me, no matter what religion I practice, as long as it is Him I worship.

Our father died in 1983 of a cerebral hemorrhage. My mother died in 1990 of congestive heart failure, one of the many complications of diabetes. They did not want to come live in this country. Wanting them here in the states had been my dream, not theirs. They were happy where and how they lived, as I am happy with myself and the family David and I have created. Like every parent, no matter the race or color, we all only want a better life for our children. I believe that in the afterlife, we will all be together again, and the artificial boundaries of nations will wash away with the tide of enlightened understanding.

Nearly thirty years after those events, when I hear news references to "illegal aliens," I wonder about the stigma we place on those now coming to this country under often precarious circumstances.

* I wonder about the thousands of individual life stories and personal histories that hang in the balance, because obtaining an employment permit or visa is often nearly impossible.

- I know first-hand what it is to be at a cultural crossroads between better economic opportunities, better education for their children, and poverty without hope.

- As a Spanish translator, I see their struggle to find a place in the world to raise a family and offer their gifts. The nature of the longing is not only to make a better life for themselves, but to make a contribution to an adopted home and community through citizenship.

- Without losing their own cultural heritage, but open to a new life, they come seeking what I have found.

I will forever be grateful for the opportunities afforded to me here in the United States to both learn and contribute—and for the unforgettable life I have made with my family.

Today and Now

I t feels like ten lifetimes since I picked coffee alongside my family in the jungles of Panamá, where life was peaceful, serene and rarely seemed affected by the outside world. I never dreamed that destiny would bring me so far away, to this frozen land, where things die in winter and rise up again in the spring to grow and blossom.

Panamá was, of course, affected by the outside world, more than I understood as a child. International interest in this narrow isthmus land that could provide a connection between the Pacific and Atlantic Oceans dated back to the 16th century. The rough terrain, unusual geology, and tropical diseases proved to be daunting challenges to both the French and the people of the United States as they struggled in the 19th and 20th centuries to survey and build the famous Panamá Canal. My tiny homeland itself became an intersecting crossroads for cultures, policies, trade, commerce, technological advancement and economic develop-ment for many nations around the world.

Panamá also became the bedrock of my first major

crossroads in life. That crossroads took me from a world of close reliance on the land, native ingenuity, and village life in the tropics to a much faster-paced, western lifestyle intimately tied with jobs in a corporate system, home mortgages, and the raising of children in a diverse culture.

There have been other crossroads of change for both me and my family where we made our home in southwest Michigan. Twenty-five years of kidney disease, two transplants, and enough health costs to nearly sink us financially have brought their own crossroads of personal growth, family commitment, and individual faith. These crises alone had the same ominous feel as that life-threatening flood from my childhood. Again and again, I survived. Again and again, we made it past the crossroads to the other side. So many times my tiny Panamá—with its world-important canal—has been a metaphor for my life. With all the challenges of overcoming impossible odds and finally celebrating an incredible accomplishment, crossroads have become central.

I never dreamed that I would live with snakes, alligators, caimans, iguana and crocodiles, animals I feared when growing up. My husband David has retired and we are planning on building a Reptile Rescue Zoo to provide a haven for unwanted pet reptiles. It will be a "mini rainforest" for people in Michigan to come and enjoy, to have a little taste of something that many here might otherwise never see. I know that this dream will come true with a lot of hard work, which both of us are willing to do. One more crossroad.

I would like to think that I live in a better world, but I am not so sure, because of the hate and violence that threatens us on so many levels. As an immigrant who adopted the United States as home through citizenship, I am conscious of the news in other countries, as well as the events in our own. The tragic attacks of 9/11 in 2001, the death of hundreds of children in Russia at the hands of terrorists in 2004, the senseless violence in the Sudan affecting hundreds of thousands of people in 2005, and the explosive conditions in the Middle East are only a few examples of the divisiveness that endangers us more than any natural enemy.

My Panamanian heritage taught me to see the crossroads and to believe in solutions, even when they might be hard-won. In sober fear, as a mother I can ask myself: How long before we eradicate one another? Will my children or grandchild see a peaceful future, when children are dying needlessly every day? In determined hope, as an American citizen and as a woman of faith, I believe we are being asked once again to lead with solutions.

I know in my heart that the peoples of the earth are at a crossroads. The many trouble-spots both at home and abroad represent the same kind of challenges the builders of the Panamá Canal faced a century ago. Can we overcome the obstacles? Is there enough technology and human intelligence to build what seems to some as impossible? Is it feasible to cross over the dangers while minimizing the loss of life? Can we devote enough of the right resources to build a passageway from one ocean to another, where there never has been one before? Can we bring cultures together?

In Panamá, the challenges included the limiting factors of resources, geology, tropical disease, and the creation of the largest humanly-constructed lake in the world, as well as many cultural and political barriers. Today, the challenges are greater than bringing technology, design and physical resources to bear in the creation of canals. But, maybe if ordinary citizens, like us, and world leaders frame our approaches to the daunting problems of racism, terrorism, and cultural misunderstanding as the most important "crossroads" of this century, we will be better equipped to make it past the threatening obstacles—whether they present themselves in the Middle East, troubled nations in Africa, and our own violent cities.

Today, the stakes are greater, but so are the goals and the promised outcome of peace. As a person of faith, I want and choose to believe that we are capable of building safe passageway, even through the dangerous waters of hate and violence. Diverse communities and nations will need to stand together. As a naturalized citizen, I believe in the power of building cultural bridges and understanding where they have not been before.

The Panamá of my childhood, where canals were built and crossroads traveled, inspires me still.

"We are children of the same Father

...all created by the same God."

—Malachi 2:10

HOW LONG BEFORE WE SEE PEACE?

FAMILY UPDATE:

- Francisco Buelvas, half-brother, died of a heart attack in 1982.

- Jose Rafael Casis is retired and lives in David, Panamá and has three children.

- Judith Aurora Echanique Lesher died in a traffic accident in Florida in 1980. She is survived by four children.

- Zarida Del Carmen Buelvas Smith (Yayin) lives in Colón, Panamá. She has four children.

- Roberto Antonio Buelvas lives in Panamá. He has three children.

- Aminta Eneida Buelvas Cobb Hamm lives in Florida. She has two children.

- Crisostomo Arnaldo Buelvas lives in Colón, Panamá. He has five children.

- Carmen Minerva Buelvas Critchlow lives in Battle Creek, Michigan. She has two children.

- Ramón Omar Buelvas lives in Colombia, South America. He has seven children.

- Cecilia Isabel Buelvas Moyers lives in Weston, Florida. She has three children.

- Zaira Maria Buelvas Ortega lives in Colón, Panamá. She has two children.

- Gloriela Imara Buelvas died in infancy.

Recipes

Whether in sorrow or celebration, the people of Panamá gather around food. I share with you some of the many recipes from my family's culture.

We all strive to live and eat in more healthy ways. In any of the following recipes for less fat or calories, use olive oil for frying and Splenda as a sweetener instead of sugar. * (See health note at end.)

REFRITO

Refrito is the base of all soups and sauces in my family. Also it is put on meats or mixed with tuna. It is usually eaten with rice. You can eat it with fried plantains or ofaldas. You can make as much or as little as you like.

Ingredients:

Green/red peppers

Onions

Cilantro or parsley

Tomatoes

Small amount of oil or spray

Salt to taste

Pepper to taste

Any other condiments you like

Heat oil. Sautee peppers, onions, cilantro and all other condiments until brown. Add tomato until boil. It will have the consistency of a sauce.

OJALDAS (ELEPHANT EARS)

In some Hispanic countries called "fried bread."

Ingredients:

2 cups flour

1 egg

1 t-spoon of oil

1 t-spoon of baking powder

Salt to taste

Water

Oil for frying

Combine all dry ingredients. Add egg and slowly add water and mix until dough is like bread. (You may have to use your hands.) Use more oil to pat the dough and leave in bowl. Cover and leave overnight. This will allow it to rise.

110

When you are ready to cook, split the dough into balls the size of golf balls. Start to slowly open them like a pizza pie. Heat oil. Fry your Ofaldas till golden brown. You can eat them that way or put peanut butter or jelly on them. As an alternative, you can sprinkle them with sugar and cinnamon on top.

PLANTAINS

Plantains are like very big bananas. There are several different ways to cook plantains, which are described below.

PATACON (FLAT PLANTAIN)

Ingredients:

1 green plantain

Oil for frying

1 flat bottom cup or glass

Peel plantain and cut in 1-inch circles.

Heat oil

Place the plantains in oil until lightly browned.

Remove from heat and with the flat cup or glass smash the plantain until flat and return to frying till golden brown. (Before and after each time, wet the bottom of the cup with the hot oil so the plantain will not stick to the cup)

Or you can cut the slices very thin and fry till golden brown without flattening them.

TAJADAS

Ingredients:

> 1 plantain (You can use green or ripe plantain.)
>
> Oil for frying
>
> Salt is optional

Peel plantain and slice diagonally.

Place plantain in heat and fry until golden brown. Sprinkle with salt.

CHOCAO (PLANTAIN PUDDING)

Ingredients:

> Very ripe plantain (almost dark)
>
> Can milk
>
> Sugar
>
> Ginger

Place plantain in a dry heated pan and slowly add milk. As you add the milk, keep mashing the plantains like mashed potatoes. Add remaining ingredients to taste. It will have the consistency of pudding and can be eaten warm or cold. You can make as much or as little as you want.

PLATANO CON POROTO (PLANTAIN AND BEANS)

Ingredients:

Ripe plantain (almost dark)

You can use any of these can beans.

Baked beans

Kidney beans

Pork and beans

Peel plantains and cut length-wise in quarters.

Place beans on a baking dish. Put plantain on top of the beans and bake for half an hour. It will have a sweet taste.

COCONUT RICE

Ingredients:

1 coconut

1 cup or rice (not instant)

2 cups of water

(This will be extracted from the coconut.)

Salt to taste

You need to peel your coconut. The easiest way to do this is to break it in half and place both halves the microwave for a few minutes. Then peel the coconut from the shell. (We use machetes.)

Cut the coconut meat into small pieces and place in a blender with water. You need to blend with enough water to extract the amount you need.

Place water in deep pan and bring to a bubbling boil with high heat, stirring so it will not boil over. After 5 minutes of bubbling boil, add your rice and salt. Let boil for another 5 minutes and turn the heat to low. Cover the pan and let it slow cook for half an hour or until rice is dry and soft.

(This will have a coconut, somewhat sweet taste.)

CHICHA VARIATIONS

CHICHA DE AVENA (OATMEAL DRINK)

Ingredients:

2 cups of oatmeal

4 cups warm water

Sugar

Cinnamon

1 Can milk

Vanilla

Put oatmeal in a pitcher and add the warm water. Let it set for about an hour. (This will extract the flavor of the oatmeal.) Put in the blender and blend once or twice. Place in a colander and extract the oatmeal from the water. You will have a juice. To the juice add the milk sugar, cinnamon and vanilla to taste.

Place in the refrigerator. You can drink this with your meals or anytime.

Refreshing Chichas can also be made out of fruits or vegetables. Follow the same preparation steps, adding sugar and milk to the main Chicha ingredients.

CHICHA DE MELON (MELON DRINK)

You can use muskmelon, watermelon or cantaloupe.

Ingredients:

Melon

Sugar

Milk

Vanilla

Put as much or as little melon as you like in a blender. Slowly add milk, enough to make juice. Add sugar and vanilla to taste.

EN SALADA DE FRUTAS

This is a tropical fruit salad. In a large bowl combine the following.

Ingredients:

    1 cup of chunk pineapple

    1 cup of mango

    1 cup of papaya

    1 cup of oranges

    1 cup of watermelon

    1 cup of coconut shavings or flakes

* Health Note: Some of these recipes are high in potassium and phospherous. As such, they are not Renal Diet friendly.

ENJOY LIFE!